REAL–LIFE
SCARY PLACES

BY TRACEY DILS

cover illustration by Roger Loveless
interior illustrations by Bob Carter

To Victoria Althoff.
You may not believe in ghosts,
but you've always believed in me.

Thanks to Richard Herrold, Jennifer Herrold,
Russell Herrold, Michael Strapp, and Michelle Spillan
for their editorial and research help.
And special thanks to Emily and Phillip
for their patience.

Published by Willowisp Press
801 94th Avenue North, St. Petersburg, Florida 33702

Copyright © 1996 by Willowisp Press,
a division of PAGES, Inc.

Printed in the United States of America

4 6 8 10 9 7 5 3

ISBN 0-87406-794-4

CONTENTS

INTRODUCTION

It's late at night. A writer sits alone in a small room in front of her computer. Beside the keyboard is a stack of yellow paper scribbled with red ink. Piled on both sides of her are books of all shapes and sizes. Some are open to creased pages. Others are open and placed face down. On the floor, between wadded-up pieces of paper, there are stacks of magazines and newspapers about the supernatural.

I am that writer, and I am pleased to present you with this collection of tales of "real-life" terror. Do ghosts really exist? Are there such things as haunted places? And what makes a ghost story "true"?

These are all questions that you, as a reader, need to decide for yourself. What is true about the places described in this book is this: they have all been the sites of documented hauntings. The people who witnessed the hauntings have either written down the account or passed the information along to writers who have written it down.

Most of the stories in this book have been retold several times. They have no doubt changed a little bit each time they have been told. Some of the characters and features of the stories may be different from the original accounts. But that's what makes a really good ghost story. Every time it is retold, it gets better and better and scarier and scarier. That's what I have tried to do with these stories. I've taken the basic account of each haunting and retold it in my own words. When the original account has provided full details, I've included them. When it hasn't, I've added a few details of my own. My research into the hauntings guided me in writing the dialogue for the stories.

Now it's your chance to get into the act. Perhaps you'll want to take these same facts about a scary place and weave them into a story of your own. Or perhaps you'll want to investigate hauntings in your hometown and then create your very own tale of terror. Whatever you do, make sure you do your research. They say the ghosts don't like it if you get the story wrong!

A storm is brewing outside my window. I hear a slight creaking in the floorboards outside my study. As I work on these stories, the creaking sounds more and more like footsteps. Suddenly, a chill fills the room. Then I feel a sensation on my back—like a hand, as if someone or something is leaning over my shoulder. There is no one there, and yet I can feel someone's hot breath on the back of my neck.

I shrug my shoulders and return to my writing. It's only the ghosts I have written about, checking my work, and making sure that I have told their tales in the most terrifying way possible.

THE
HORROR
OF
BERKELEY
SQUARE

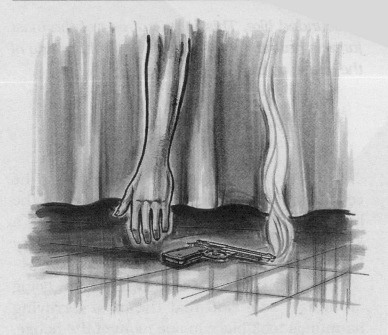

STORIES *about haunted houses have been told for hundreds of years. Some hauntings are just a bunch of scary noises—footsteps, groans, cries, or screams. In some cases, the ghosts play tricks. They might rearrange the furniture or play a musical instrument in the middle of the night. In other hauntings, the ghosts actually appear, sometimes as lights or as wispy, shadowlike shapes.*

There are some hauntings that are so horrible that no one lives to tell what they looked

...s *true of one of the most*
...t *the world—the haunting of*
...*keley Square.*

Sir Robert didn't believe in ghosts. And he certainly didn't believe in the horror of the house on Berkeley Square. After all, he was a knight and this was nineteenth-century London. He had no time for such nonsense.

Oh, he'd heard the stories that were going around. It was said that the most terrifying hauntings took place in one room of the house. In fact, people said, a young servant girl had gone mad after she spent the night there. After that fateful night, she was able to say only one phrase. "Don't let it touch me," she murmured over and over. The story had to be true, people said. It had even been reported in the newspapers.

There was also a story about two poor sailors who found themselves with no place to stay one foggy night. They had stumbled upon the deserted house and decided to sleep there. They built a fire in the fireplace and settled down for the night when they heard it—a scratching and panting sound outside the walls, as if a wild animal was trying to get in.

Then they saw it—a horrible, ghostlike creature, not quite animal, not quite human. The thing snarled and stretched its sharp, bloody claws toward them.

One of the sailors escaped through the window. From the street, he heard his friend scream again and again. He ran to find the police.

When he returned with the authorities, there was no sign of his friend in the room. Finally, they found him on the back steps. His neck had been broken. On his face was a look of unspeakable horror.

"Poppycock." That's what Sir Robert said when he heard the stories about the house on Berkeley Square. He was eating dinner with a group of his friends. When they kept telling more and more stories, each one more horrible than the one before, Sir Robert decided it was up to him to prove once and for all that there were no such things as haunted houses.

He would spend the night in the Berkeley Square house, he told his friends. In fact, he would spend the night in the very room where the servant girl had been driven to insanity.

His friends begged him not to do it. But Sir Robert would not change his mind.

Mr. Benson, the owner of the house, wasn't too excited about the idea, but Sir Robert convinced him that nothing would happen. Sir Robert said he would take his gun with him, just in case. And he would ask his friends to sleep in the room downstairs. They would be on hand to rescue him, should he need it.

So the plan was set in motion. Sir Robert, chuckling under his breath, headed up to the cursed room after a hearty dinner one night. Before he left, he assured his friends that if he saw anything—anything at all—he would pull the cord beside his bed to ring a bell. Then, he said, rolling his eyes, they could all come running and rescue him.

Only forty-five minutes later, something did happen. Sir Robert's friends heard the jangle of the bell throughout the halls. They headed toward the room, dreading what they might find there.

As they ran up the stairs, an unearthly scream echoed through the hallways. Then a lone gunshot rang out.

They approached the room thinking that Sir Robert had killed whatever was in the room. They were sure that he had finally solved the mystery of the Berkeley Square horror.

But what they found was something far different. Sir Robert lay sprawled across the bed. His eyes bulged from their sockets in a look of terror. His mouth was wide open as if he had been trying to scream.

Sir Robert was dead. The gun lay on the floor, just below his limp hand. His friends gasped. The plan must have gone wrong. Someone must have killed Sir Robert with his own gun!

But there was no gunshot wound anywhere on his body—just a single gunshot hole in the wall surrounded by a perfect circle of black soot. Sir Robert may have *tried* to shoot whoever—or whatever—was after him. But the sight he had seen must have frightened him to death.

Today, you can visit the house of Berkeley Square in London, England, if you dare. The house has been turned into a bookstore and whatever was haunting its halls has apparently left. No hauntings or ghost sightings have been reported for a hundred years.

THE
TERROR
OF
EMILY'S
BRIDGE

WHY do ghosts return to certain places time and time again? Some spirits may return to have their revenge on the living. Others may return to warn the living of some danger or to give them an important message. But perhaps the saddest hauntings of them all involve ghosts who have come back from the dead to search for their long-lost sweethearts, sweethearts the ghosts were somehow unable to be with while they were living. Powerful forces send them on their endless searches, forces that are sometimes too strong for the living to ignore.

The story that follows is based on several tales that are told about a haunted bridge in Stowe, Vermont. In all these tales, the ghost of Emily Smith searches desperately for her bridegroom on the bridge. Emily weaves a powerful spell as she searches for her lost love.

It is an ordinary bridge over an ordinary creek. Some people call the old covered bridge Gold Brook Bridge. Others know it as Stowe Hollow Bridge. But most of the locals in the small ski town of Stowe, Vermont, call it Emily's Bridge. And most of them swear that the ghost of Emily Smith has been haunting its dark passageway since the late 1800s.

David Belton had heard stories about Emily's Bridge since he was a young boy, but he didn't believe any of them. There were those who said that Emily would chase people across the bridge. Some said that horses were spooked at the edge of the bridge and would not pass through. Still others claimed to hear moans or screams. Ghostly lights had been reported on the edge of the creek on either side of the bridge. David thought they were ridiculous stories. After all, Emily Smith had been dead for nearly a hundred years. The bridge that bore her name was a rickety old covered bridge from another time. Some of the townspeople claimed it was the oldest covered bridge in the country. Built in 1844, the bridge had a rich history. It was no wonder that people told stories about it.

Even though David didn't believe the stories, he still didn't feel comfortable visiting the bridge at night. He wondered, then, why he had allowed his buddies to convince him to go to the bridge that first Saturday in April. The date was significant. According to his friends, that was the night that Emily Smith had died by jumping off the bridge that came to bear her name. David hadn't been able to come up with an excuse that didn't make him sound like a complete chicken, so he had agreed to go. And now he sat in his friend's old Volkswagen bus on the way to the bridge, listening to stories about the long-lost Emily Smith.

"They say she was stood up on her wedding day," one of his friends said. "Her fiancé never showed up at church. So she climbed on a horse, headed to the bridge, and then she and the horse both jumped off the bridge."

"No. That's not how it goes," said another boy. "You're right about her being stood up at the altar, but she didn't mean to kill herself. She took off in a wagon at full speed, hoping to track the jerk down. Then, when she reached the bridge, she was going too fast. She crashed off the bridge, wagon and all."

"I heard it differently," a third friend said. "I heard that Emily's bridegroom was killed on the bridge on the way to the ceremony. It was his wagon that crashed off the bridge. When Emily heard the news, she was so upset she rushed to the bridge and jumped off from the exact spot where his wagon had fallen."

David shook his head. *Crazy stories*, he thought. *This just shows how ghost stories can get out of hand.*

"Whatever happened," the first friend continued, "her ghost still wears her wedding dress. They say she's still looking for her bridegroom. Maybe she'll find him tonight."

"Yeah, right," David chuckled. "Like I really believe this garbage."

Then, ahead of him in the clearing by the creek, he saw the bridge. *An ordinary bridge,* he assured himself. *Now let's cross it and get out of here.*

There was nothing unusual at the edge of the creek. No weird lights, no moans, no screams. As the wheels of the car rattled across the bridge, absolutely nothing unusual happened. The driver stopped the car in the middle of the bridge, pretending that it had stalled, but he didn't fool David or the rest of the guys.

"See, no ghost!" David said. "I told you guys this was crazy—"

David stopped in midsentence. The car began shaking back and forth. All at once, the four boys reached for the locks on the doors.

The car kept shaking, first a gentle rolling, then more violently. It was as if someone or something was trying to throw them off the bridge. The faces of David's companions turned a greenish shade. And David himself felt his heart drop to his socks.

Then David saw it—a face at the window. It appeared only for the briefest second, but it was clearly the face of a woman peering at him from beneath a bridal veil. David's heart began racing in terror. Suddenly another feeling came over him, a feeling David couldn't quite describe.

There was something about the look on the face of the ghostly apparition. It was a look of sorrow, painful sorrow. Her eyes, flashing a deep green in the darkness, revealed intense longing. Even in his brief moment of terror, David felt his heart go out to her. The look of grief was almost more than he could bear. It was the kind of sadness that drew him in, that made him want to comfort her. It was a look that actually made him think about opening his door and going to her. It was the strangest feeling David had ever had. Then he felt his hand reaching for the door lock. David felt his body strangely pulled toward hers.

Then the shaking suddenly stopped and the image of the ghostly bride faded behind the window glass. A voice inside David's head begged her to stay, but the image had gone.

David pulled his hand back and sighed with relief. The strange, sweet sensation of longing for Emily Smith had passed.

"D-d-did you—?" his buddy was stammering from the front seat.

"See her?" David said, trying to control his

own voice. "Yeah, I saw her. Now let's get out of here!"

But David didn't have to say any more. His buddy started the car and floored it. The car practically shot out of Emily's Bridge.

When they reached the other side, they heard a sound that would ring forever in their ears. An unearthly scream, a woman's scream, echoed through the bridge. Then a loud splash was heard from the creek below.

It seemed that Emily had failed to find her bridegroom once again and had drowned her sorrows in the waters of Gold Brook. Only David, the sweat beading on his brow, knew just how close she had come.

Emily's Bridge, located a couple of miles north of the center of Stowe, Vermont, is a great spot for a picnic on a warm summer's day. If you take a trip to Emily's Bridge, you'll want to head home long before nightfall. In the darkness, Emily still searches for her bridegroom, and you wouldn't want to find yourself a victim of her irresistible charms.

THE
HAUNTED
CRYPT
OF
BARBADOS

GRAVEYARDS, *crypts, burial vaults. On dark, foggy nights, these are the places where our imaginations can work overtime and create ghostly images that aren't really there. We may think we see mysterious lights among the headstones. We may suddenly think we smell a strange odor or feel an unseen hand on our back. Or we may see a dim shadow that somehow becomes a ghost in our minds.*

Too many people saw what went on in the burial crypt of the Chase family for it to be written off to runaway imaginations. What happened there happened more than once. And whoever—or whatever—was responsible for these horrible disturbances must have possessed superhuman power.

Early in the 1800s, Colonel Thomas Chase brought his family from England to live on Barbados, a small tropical island in the middle of the Caribbean Sea. It wasn't the island's gentle trade winds or white sandy beaches that attracted the colonel to this place. It was his need for power—absolute, total control.

Barbados was a place where Chase could live like a king. West Indian slaves would be at his beck and call at every moment. Also, because he was so far away from English society, no one back home would ever know when he let his ugly temper get out of control. So what if he directed violent, angry outbursts at his family members? There would be no one else around to hear his bouts of rage. Barbados was the perfect place for the likes of Thomas Chase.

He built his mansion first, high on a cliff overlooking the ocean. But the mansion wasn't enough for the colonel. He needed a symbol to show that he and his family meant to stay on this island and make it their home. When he saw a burial vault that looked like a small house made of carved coral and stone, he knew that he had to make it the Chase family crypt. All the members of the Chase family, he declared, would be placed in this crypt after their deaths. So he bought it, not knowing that his soul—and the souls of his relatives—would find no peace there.

The colonel quickly established his reputation as an ill-tempered master who was cruel to his slaves. He was barely kinder to his own family. As a parent, he let anger get in the way of love, yelling and screaming at his children instead of playing with them or helping them to learn new things.

It didn't take long for bad things to start happening to the members of the Chase family in their new home. Shortly after Chase had settled his family in this tropical paradise, his wife's aunt, a Mrs. Goddard, fell ill with fever and died. It was a sudden death, the kind that sometimes happens to those not used to warmer climates. After a showy funeral, Mrs. Goddard's casket was placed in the empty family crypt. A large slab of concrete was placed over the opening to the vault and cemented in place. Only a few months later, Chase's infant daughter died mysteriously. The slab was opened, and her tiny coffin was placed alongside her aunt's. Then the slab was cemented into place again.

In spite of his misfortune, few people felt sorry for Chase. In fact, among the natives it was whispered that his cruelty had brought on evil spirits they called "duppies" that would plague his family forever.

To make matters worse, instead of grieving his losses, Colonel Chase became even more ill-tempered and unreasonable. He was particularly hard on his eldest daughter, Dorcas. According to Chase, Dorcas could not do anything right.

Four short years later, Dorcas Chase died. Some say she committed suicide by starving herself to death. Others say that she died of a broken heart. Whatever the cause, the Chase family gathered for another funeral. They placed Dorcas's casket in the carved family crypt next to the infant and Mrs. Goddard. The crypt was sealed and the remaining family members went back to walking on eggshells whenever they came near Thomas Chase.

Then Chase himself died suddenly. It was rumored that he was so upset about Dorcas's death that he had committed suicide too. Among the natives, a different rumor was going around. The duppies, they said, had done their dreadful work again.

Family members gathered at yet another funeral, this one less sad than the others. It wasn't that they didn't mourn Chase's death. It was just that they were relieved to know they would no longer be victims of his rage.

When they opened the crypt to place Chase's body inside, the family gasped at the scene before them. All the heavy lead caskets were in disarray, as if they had been tossed around the crypt by some unseen force. The baby's casket was in the weirdest position of all—upside down at the opposite end of the crypt from where it had originally been placed.

After they gathered their wits about them, the family members figured out what must have happened. Vandals must have gotten into the tomb. But how could they? The stone slab that covered the opening had been sealed tight. Rather than consider that the crypt was perhaps as cursed as the family had been, the remaining Chases somehow convinced themselves that the disorder in the crypt had been the work of common vandals. They had workmen set the coffins back in order. They also ordered that sand be spread on the floor so that they could identify the intruders by their footprints should they return.

It wasn't until four years later that the crypt was reopened, this time for the burial of yet another infant. When the slab was opened, a task that took the strength of four workmen, the caskets were again found scattered around the crypt—some upside down, some lying on their sides. There was not a single footprint or marking in the white sand that covered the floor.

Once more, the coffins were put in their proper places. And again, when the tomb was reopened, the coffins were found scattered randomly around the crypt. The entire crypt was re-examined, but there seemed to be no logical explanation. The natives renewed their whispers about duppies. The English people who inhabited the island came up with their own ghostly theories. Perhaps, they said, Chase's own family would not receive his soul, even in death. After all, that's when the whole business had begun—just after Chase died. Others said that this was Dorcas's way of protesting having to share a crypt with her cruel father.

Lord Combermere didn't believe in such nonsense. He had bought a home in the neighborhood of the crypt in the 1820s and was tired of the rumors and the silly native superstitions. He would prove once and for all that the monkey business in the crypt was not the work of unhappy spirits or duppies.

He had the Chase crypt sealed with new mortar, a process he himself witnessed. He even had the governor make his mark in the seal, and he invited other townspeople to do the same. Any crack in the seal would be a sure sign that the slab had been opened and that someone had gone inside. Nine months later, he promised, he would have the crypt opened again. He was certain the coffins would be in the positions in which they had been left. Nothing would be able to get into the crypt.

When the nine months had passed, the entire population of the island gathered around to see what had happened inside the tomb. The mortar was unbroken and all the official seals were untouched.

But when Lord Combermere ordered several of the workmen to remove the slab, it did not budge. It took twelve men to move it, and even then it moved only a few inches to let a single man inside. Once one of the workmen entered, he discovered why the slab had been so stubborn.

A single heavy coffin had been placed upside down against the stone slab. And every other coffin had been moved as well. The smaller ones had been slammed so hard against the tomb's walls that they had made dents in the stone. The other coffins lay every which way. Some had even been stacked on top of each other.

The remaining members of the Chase family had had enough. They ordered all the coffins removed and buried in separate underground graves. The Chase family vault is empty to this day, and the mystery of the moving coffins has never been solved.

If you ever have the opportunity to go to the lovely island of Barbados, you can visit the abandoned tomb of the Chase family and try to imagine what tremendous force might have moved those coffins. You may even be able to convince a native to tell you his or her own version of the story, for this is a tale that is still passed from generation to generation on the island.

THE
BLOODY
TOWER
OF
LONDON

BLOODY beheadings, unspeakable acts of hideous torture, horrifyingly violent murders—the places that have witnessed events like these seem forever cursed. The victims of such cruelty often never leave the scenes of their gruesome deaths, preferring instead to haunt the living, to remind others of their bloody end, or to take revenge on those who harmed them.

The Tower of London may be the bloodiest spot in all of England. Today, the tower is a tourist attraction, but for most of its history, this *magnificent fortress on the Thames River was a prison and the site of more executions and murders than perhaps any other on earth. It is no wonder that those who died there return time and time again, screaming, crying, or simply wandering the tower's hallways in silent agony, so that all who enter will know of their pain.*

It was a respectable post, the first this young sentry had held. For some reason, the position as guard of the entrance to a small room in the Tower of London had been open for some time. The captain of the sentries said that he just couldn't find the right person for the job. That seemed a little strange, the sentry thought. After all, there must be plenty of people qualified for the position. Whatever the reason, the young man was honored to be given the opportunity to take over the night watch.

Of course, one couldn't be English and not have heard a little bit about the history of the tower itself. Construction of the tower began in

1066. Hundreds—maybe thousands—of enemies of the crown were executed there over the nine hundred years that it had stood on the banks of the Thames River. Two young princes—Edward V and his brother Richard of York—were murdered there in the 1400s. The youngsters probably were killed by their uncle, Richard III, so that he could take the throne.

Then there was Margaret, the countess of Salisbury. It took five blows from the executioner's ax to accomplish her beheading. It was said she escaped in the middle of it all, forcing the executioner to chase her around the room with his bloody ax.

Perhaps the most famous execution took place in the 1500s. King Henry VIII had divorced his first wife; now he wanted to be rid of the second. But another divorce was out of the question. His people wouldn't stand for it.

So Henry came up with a plan. He accused his wife, Anne Boleyn, of treason and suggested that she had been seeing other men. The trial was short and, to no one's great surprise, Anne was found guilty. She was sentenced to death by beheading.

As heartless and cruel as Henry was, he

couldn't deny his queen her last wish. Young Anne was terrified of dying a painful death at the hands of an awkward executioner. So Henry brought an axman from France, someone skilled at beheading. The executioner even brought with him a special sword so that Anne's death could be swift and painless.

When the execution was complete, Anne's headless body was put in an old chest and buried quickly, without ceremony, in a chapel in the tower.

If the young sentry was aware of these stories, he didn't let them bother him. This was the middle of the 1800s, after all, and all of that had happened long ago. He knew how important his job was. The tower wasn't only a place of bloody execution. The crown jewels were kept there too. If a thief broke in, he could end up with priceless treasures, treasures that the royal family had kept safe for years.

And so the sentry stood at his post night after night, always alert to danger, always on the lookout for anyone who might pass down this particular hallway after breaking into the tower.

On one such night, he was standing at his post, watching for anything unusual. He was a bit tired. He and his buddies had spent a few hours at the pub before he reported for work. In the wee hours of the night, just before dawn, the sentry heard what sounded like footsteps, light taps really, echoing down the hallway. He shook his head, sure that the sounds were his imagination. Perhaps the ale was still in his system.

Then he saw something strange: an eerie glow at the end of the hallway. As he watched, a faint figure, almost like a shadow, came walking toward him through the glowing light. He couldn't quite make out what the figure was wearing, but from where he stood, it looked like a long brown dress. On the figure's head was some sort of bonnet or headdress.

The sentry closed his eyes. I must be very tired, he thought. But when he opened his eyes, the figure was still there, coming closer and closer. It *was* a bonnet on her head, but he couldn't make out her face.

Taking a deep breath, he cried, "Who goes there?"

The figure took another step toward him.

The sentry felt his heart beating wildly as he cowered against the cold stone wall of the tower. He closed his eyes again, for a few seconds this time, trying to wipe the image he had seen out of his mind.

When he opened them again, the figure was standing right in front of him. He drew in a deep breath and forced himself to look the figure straight in the eyes. Only the figure had no eyes. The figure had no face. Underneath the bonnet, the figure had no head, only a bloody stump of a neck.

From the depths of his heart, the sentry summoned all of the courage he could manage. He had a bayonet on the end of his rifle and, his hands shaking, he stabbed the figure.

The bayonet went right through the figure's body without harming her.

The sentry screamed. His horrible wail echoed through the tower walls as he fell to his knees. Then he fell unconscious on the tower's cold, hard floor.

The next thing he felt was someone shaking him, shaking him so hard his teeth chattered. Reluctantly, the sentry opened one eye. It was his boss, the captain of the sentries. And he didn't look very happy.

"Sleeping on the job, huh?" the captain grunted. "You're dismissed from your post. And, in a week's time, you'll face a court-martial."

The sentry tried to explain what had happened, but the captain scoffed at his story. When the court-martial was held, the sentry was sure he would face a prison sentence. But he knew he at least had to try to explain himself to the judge.

He told the story of his last night watch, every horrible detail of it. But the judge just shook his head. The sentry knew he was doomed.

Then, as the judge was about to pass sentence, two men stepped forward.

"Please, your honor, might we say a few words?" said one of the men.

The judge raised his eyebrows. "Have your say, but be quick about it."

"This sentry, what he has said is true."

"Yes," said the other man. "He is telling the truth."

"This is preposterous!" said the judge. "What on earth could he have seen?"

"It's bloody Anne," said the shorter of the two men. "It is the ghost of Anne Boleyn."

"It was in that small room that she was imprisoned before her execution."

The judge raised his eyebrows once again. "And how do you know this?"

"Because," said the shorter of the two men, his bloodshot eyes round, "we were once sentries in that very spot."

"And," said the other, his voice shaking, "we saw her too."

The young sentry was set free, but he would not return to his post in the tower. That job would be left to whoever dared to take it.

Today, you can visit the Tower of London, the site of some of history's most gruesome deaths. Your tour guide will be glad to tell you his or her own version of these—and other— hauntings. And if you're lucky, you may even encounter one of the tower ghosts yourself.

THE
BLOODY
WATERS
OF
DISAPPOINTMENT
ISLAND

FOR as long as sailors have been sailing the seas, they have told tales of mermaids, sea monsters, and ghostly phantom ships. Perhaps the tales are yarns spun to pass the long hours aboard ship. Maybe they are the result of a runaway imagination brought on by the sea's hypnotic rhythms. Or they might be superstitions that have been passed from one generation of sailors to another until they seem true.

Sometimes, though, things happen at sea that cannot be explained. And there are places in the ocean where the sea's mysterious forces *seem to take over, claiming sailor after sailor as their victims. Disappointment Island just south of Hawaii is one such place. The waters around the island are supposedly more haunted than any others on earth. Many of these hauntings involve a ghostly ship believed to be the legendary* Flying Dutchman. *Whenever the ship appears, it brings terror along with it. The story that follows is a retelling of one of the* Flying Dutchman *hauntings.*

Admiral Lord Canwilliam was tired of hearing the stories about the *Flying Dutchman,* a ship that supposedly sailed the high seas bringing disaster to whoever saw it. He didn't believe the stories himself, and he didn't want the crew members of the *Bacchante* wasting their time telling tales to each other. After all, they had important work to do.

The year was 1881, and they were headed from New Zealand to Disappointment Island, just south of Hawaii, in search of the lost ship the *Ulysses S. Grant.* The ship had been carrying more than a million dollars worth of gold dust and had sunk with its treasure below a cavern off the coast of the island. There were rumors that the *Flying Dutchman* had been seen just before the wreck occurred. There were even those who said the *Dutchman* was responsible for the shipwreck. There were so many sailors who believed the tales of the *Flying Dutchman* that it was hard to convince them otherwise.

The legend of the *Flying Dutchman* tells of a Dutch ship that had taken to the high seas in the 1500s under the command of a Captain Vanderdecken. It had experienced calm weather, but as it rounded the Cape of Good Hope around the tip of Africa, a horrible storm blew up. Huge waves crashed over the ship's side. Strong winds ripped at her sails.

The *Flying Dutchman* crew, fearing they would be lost at sea, begged the captain to find a safe port. The captain refused. He claimed they were cowards, every one of them. Danger was what sailing was all about. There would be no peaceful passage for his crew; they would have to tough it out like true sailors. The more the crew begged, the more steadfast the captain became, even laughing at their request. He even went so far as to shoot one of the crew members who begged the hardest. Then he threw the man's body overboard.

Suddenly, a strange glowing form appeared on deck in front of the captain. Instead of being frightened, the captain just laughed.

The form approached him and spoke. "Captain, you are a fool," the glowing figure said.

"A fool I might be," the captain replied. "I do not want a peaceful passage. I want the excitement of a storm like this one."

The captain then reached for his pistol, but the gun exploded in his hands.

The figure continued, "Your gun is no match for my power. And, since you love the high seas so much, you will never leave them. You will forever sail on this ship, bringing ruin to all who see you." That curse explains why the *Flying Dutchman* has been seen ever since.

But Admiral Canwilliam wasn't the only one on board the *Bacchante* who thought such tales of the ship were nonsense. Prince George, who would later become King George V of England, was part of the crew too. George was too sensible a man to believe in ghost ships and the like. He shared the admiral's belief that the crew members had to stay focused on the task at hand. They had to recover the lost gold from the sunken ship.

The morning they arrived in the calm waters off Disappointment Island, they saw a sight that made them change their minds. Just before dawn, three sailors on watch spotted a ship just off the port bow. The ship seemed to be bathed in a red light. Two of the sailors went to report what they had seen, leaving the third one behind to watch the ship. When they returned, there was no sign of the ship. The unfortunate sailor, though, had fallen from his perch in the crow's nest. His body lay broken and bleeding on the ship's deck. He was the *Bacchante*'s first victim of the *Flying Dutchman*.

The admiral refused to believe that the sailors had seen the ship or that it had anything to do with the dead sailor. Although the death was tragic, it was only an unfortunate accident. Furthermore, he said, it showed what could happen if the men allowed themselves to be distracted by ridiculous stories of ghost ships.

After the sailor was buried at sea, the admiral organized a party of three crew members to go ashore to search for signs of the wrecked ship. The three never made it. As soon as they were a hundred yards or so away from the *Bacchante,* their tiny rowboat capsized, overturned by a huge wave that seemed to come out of nowhere. After the boat overturned, the ocean waters where it had last been seen churned with blood for several hours.

The admiral claimed it was a whirlpool, and that these things happen at sea. "Tomorrow," he said resolutely, "we will try again to reach the island."

The following morning, the *Flying Dutchman* reappeared, and this time it was the young prince who witnessed its ghostly voyage. In his log, he recorded seeing a ship that seemed to glow in the dawn's light. This time the ship appeared about two hundred yards away. Again it was bathed in a red light, but its riggings, mast, and sails were plain to see.

The prince realized that the legend of the *Flying Dutchman* was no legend. It was a curse—one that would do the ship in if they didn't leave the area at once.

The admiral resisted but eventually gave in to the prince's pleas. The *Bacchante* headed back to the nearest port without finding the sunken ship or the treasures in its hold.

But the *Flying Dutchman* had not yet finished its work. Several of the men reported seeing the ship following them as they approached the harbor. Once again the admiral scoffed at their stories, but he soon learned just how evil the phantom ship was.

The moment they arrived in port, the admiral was struck with a strange illness. He grew feverish and then delirious. As he tried to make his way off the ship, he stumbled and fell into the sea. His body disappeared beneath the black waters. Moments later, the ocean churned red, with the admiral's blood this time. The *Flying Dutchman* had worked its wicked magic once again.

The Flying Dutchman *continues its doomed voyages in and around Disappointment Island to this day. If you have a chance to visit this long stretch of water just south of Hawaii, be sure to look over your shoulder. If you see a ship following you, it may be time to look for a safe port, lest you too become a victim of the ship's deadly curse.*

THE CURSED SKULL OF KILNER MANOR

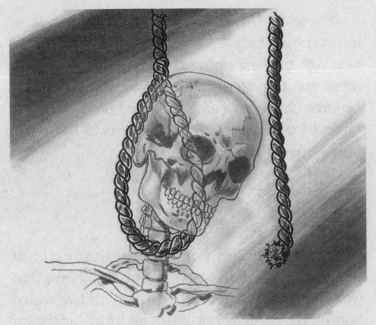

$\mathcal{S}$OME houses just seem to attract ghosts who move in and stay forever and ever. Other places become haunted when a particular object is brought in. The object may carry an awful curse with it. Or it may have a gruesome past of its own, a past that the object carries with it into the present. Sometimes the hauntings stop once it becomes "comfortable" in its new surroundings. In other cases, however, the object's forces are so evil that the house itself cannot contain them.

There may be a lesson in these kinds of hauntings. Perhaps these cursed objects are best left in their rightful places. That's exactly what the Englishman Dr. Kilner learned when he brought a special souvenir home from the hospital where he worked. It was a lesson in pure terror he would never forget.

Dr. John Kilner had to have that skull. It wasn't that he didn't have plenty of others, that was for sure. After all, Kilner had a weird hobby. He collected skulls of all kinds and kept them nicely polished in ebony boxes in his library. But this particular skull was special and his collection wouldn't be complete without it. He decided to find a way to steal it away from the hospital where he worked.

The skull had once been the head of a certain William Corder, a man who had committed a horrible crime. As the story went, Corder had agreed to marry a young girl named Maria Marten. Instead of marrying her, though, he murdered her in cold blood in an old barn just north of town. Then he buried her body beneath the floor of the barn.

Corder was later caught, tried, and sentenced to be hanged. On August 11, 1828, the entire village came out to Bury St. Edmunds, the prison where he had been kept, to watch his execution. The rope from which Corder was hanged was said to have healing properties, and pieces of it were sold for an outrageous price. After the hanging, Corder's body was publicly dissected and more than five thousand people filed by to see the murderer's grisly remains. Parts of the scalp were dried and sold to the highest bidders. The skeleton was taken to West Suffolk Hospital, where it would be used to teach anatomy to medical students.

Some time later, Kilner first saw the skull and knew that he had to make it his own. One night, after most of the other doctors had gone home, he took the skull from the skeleton and put another skull in its place. He then strode casually out of the hospital with the skull of the murderer hidden underneath his cloak.

Once he was home, he put the skull in an ebony box and placed it with the others on a shelf in his library. The doctor smiled happily at his collection. Finally, it was complete.

From that moment on, however, there was no peace in the Kilner manor. It was as if the skull itself held the spirit of the evil William Corder.

The disturbances were small ones at first, easily explained away. Doors banged shut without warning. Kilner decided it was probably the wind. Candles blew out and windows opened and closed. Again, Kilner thought it was just a draft of air blowing through the old house.

Then Kilner saw something he couldn't explain away. A stranger appeared in the library just below the shelf where the skull had been placed. The doctor rubbed his eyes and, when he opened them, the stranger had disappeared. Kilner thought his imagination had been playing tricks on him. But later the maid reported seeing the same stranger in the kitchen. The gardener saw the stranger standing in the garden with his gaze riveted on the window of the library.

Soon the whole house seemed taken over by some sort of mysterious force. Wherever Kilner went, he heard footsteps behind him. He felt a hot breath on the back of his neck. The doors of the house banged shut and flew open with a more violent force. Then he heard the screaming—horrible wailing that continued off and on every night. The screaming came from the library where the skull was kept.

Dr. Kilner was at his wits' end. He knew the source of the haunting was the skull, but he didn't really want to get rid of his prize trophy. Besides, he didn't know what to do with it. He couldn't return it to Corder's skeleton. He had polished the skull to a pearl-like sheen. It would look out of place and then he would have to admit that he had stolen it. He decided that if he could just wait it out, maybe the hauntings would stop or at least slow down. Maybe the skull or whatever was haunting the skull would decide that it liked its new surroundings.

Then something happened to show Kilner how wrong he was. One night he heard a rattling sound coming from the library. With a candle in hand, he began to investigate. As he came close to the library door, he stopped dead in his tracks. He couldn't believe what he was seeing. In the flickering light of the candle, a bony white hand seemed to float in the air, beckoning him to follow. He swallowed hard and made his way to the entrance of the library.

Suddenly, a loud explosion like a firecracker sounded from within the library's walls. The explosion was followed by a gust of icy-cold air. The ghostly hand disappeared. But the sight that Kilner saw in the library was more horrible than anything he could have ever imagined.

The ebony box that had held Corder's skull was smashed into hundreds of pieces on the library floor. Kilner frantically looked around for the skull. He gasped when he saw it.

There it was, on a shelf—a different shelf from where it once had been. In fact, somehow the skull had moved to a locked cabinet clear on the other side of the room. There, on its face, was the most evil grin Kilner had ever seen.

Kilner knew then that the skull could not stay in his house a second longer. After some quick research, he located Mr. C. F. Hopkins, an official at the prison where Corder had been executed. The two men figured that if the skull were returned to the site of Corder's death, it might finally be at peace.

While Corder's skull did not cause mischief at the prison like it had at Kilner's home, it did bring great misfortune to the Hopkins family. Hopkins and other family members were plagued by a sudden illness. They suffered financial problems. And everyone in the family seemed to fall victim to all kinds of weird accidents. It was only after Hopkins had Corder's skull buried in a Christian ceremony that it seemed to rest in peace. Once that was done, Kilner and Hopkins were able to prosper in their careers and home lives.

You can see portions of Corder's preserved scalp and read about his trial in a special museum in Bury St. Edmund's, England. His skeleton is still being used to teach anatomy at West Suffolk General Hospital—minus the skull, of course!

THE
GHOSTLY
REVENGE
AT
FORT
TICONDEROGA

IN Scotland, there is no greater bond of loyalty than that between family members. Extended families known as clans have defended their honor through centuries in bloody battles.

Likewise, a promise is a sacred oath to a Scotsman, and it is not to be broken. But what happens when a promise and family loyalty collide?

For the members of one Scottish family, this collision resulted in a horrible curse, a curse that

71

extended from the Scottish moors to a fort along the Hudson River in what is now upstate New York.

It was a particularly nasty night on the moor. The year was 1757, and Duncan Campbell had just settled himself in front of a blazing fire inside his manor in the town of Inverawe, Scotland. Campbell had been a soldier but had retired from the army to lead a quiet life in the country. At least he had thought it would be quiet.

Just as he had begun to warm up in front of the fire, he heard a strange sound at his front door. It sounded like a man screaming for help, but it was difficult to hear over the roar of the wind. Duncan raced to the door to see who was there.

When he opened the heavy oak door of the manor, he was shocked by what he saw. There stood a man nearly covered from head to toe with fresh blood.

"Help me!" the man begged. "A pack of men

jumped me just down the road. I turned my sword on them and killed the tallest one. Now the others are after me. You must help."

Duncan took one look at the fear in the blood-covered stranger's eyes and knew he couldn't deny him shelter. After all, the man seemed to be telling the truth. And, if he had indeed committed the murder in self-defense, then he deserved to be kept safe from further violence until the authorities could be called.

"I will hide you here," Duncan said. "You needn't fear. Follow me."

The man looked at him in disbelief.

"Come!" Duncan said. "You have my word that no one will harm you."

"Your word?" the man asked.

"I swear by my sword. Now let's go!"

Duncan led the man up one staircase, and then another, and another, until they reached the attic of the old manor. There he led him to a secret room behind a closet. "You can hide here," he said. "No one knows about this room. You'll be safe."

The man's look of relief was all the gratitude that Duncan needed. Certain that the fugitive would be safe, Duncan headed downstairs.

Just as he reached the bottom step of the last staircase, he heard a loud clamor at his front door.

Three men were at the door, and Duncan could tell from the looks on their faces that they were out for the fugitive's blood.

Duncan recognized one of the men from the village. The man was a good friend of Duncan's cousin Donald. "What is the meaning of this?" Duncan asked. "Why have you come to my house so late at night?"

"It is your cousin Donald," the man answered. "He has been murdered and we are seeking the villain responsible."

"Yes," cried another. "The wretch was seen heading this way."

Duncan felt his heart drop. The man he hid was Donald's murderer, and yet he had sworn on his sword to protect him. Duncan couldn't go back on his word. Now that he knew that Donald was involved, he knew that the man's story could well be true. Donald had a violent temper and he often let it get the best of him. In fact, he had bragged about attacking and beating travelers along the road, just for the fun of it. Perhaps this murder was, as the man had said, committed in self-defense.

Duncan took a deep breath. "He is not here," he lied. "I have seen no such man."

The men of the search party looked at him doubtfully. "I have seen no such man," Duncan repeated. "Now leave me in peace!"

The small troop departed, muttering curses as they left.

Duncan couldn't sleep that night. Plagued with guilty thoughts, he tossed and turned in his bed. He knew that he owed it to his cousin to turn the criminal in. But he had given the murderer his word. Duncan desperately wanted to believe him.

He was still deciding what he should do when he heard a strange sound. He couldn't quite make out what the sound was, but it sounded a bit like the word *Inverawe,* the name of the village that had once been home to all of the Campbell clan. It was a tradition in Scotland to call members of the clan by the name of their hometown. The voice became louder, more insistent, and it seemed to be coming from the other side of the bedroom door. Campbell rose from his bed and flung the door open.

There, just outside the door, stood his cousin Donald Campbell—only it wasn't the Donald Campbell Duncan remembered. His face was strangely white and his eyes shone an eerie yellow in the darkness. Duncan knew in a flash that he was seeing the ghost of his departed cousin.

"Inverawe!" The voice was coming from the ghost. "Inverawe!" it said. "You hide my murderer in this house."

Duncan Campbell wanted to protest, to explain his predicament, but when he tried to speak, he discovered that his tongue could not form the words.

"Hide him not!" the voice shouted angrily. "You must kill him. Blood for blood. It is the Campbell way."

Then, as suddenly as the ghost appeared, it vanished into thin air.

Trembling in fear, Duncan knew what he must do. He couldn't bring himself to kill the pitiful man, but he knew that he must remove him from the Campbell manor. He dressed quickly and went to the attic to fetch the murderer. In the misty dawn, he led him to a cave far from the house. "You must hide here,"

Duncan said. "You are no longer safe in my house."

The man nodded. The cave was not as warm as the attic room, but it would do. Duncan left him there with plenty of provisions and hurried back across the moor to his manor by the sea.

Duncan was relieved. That night, his eyes closed easily and he soon fell into a deep sleep. His peaceful sleep didn't last long, however. The ghostly figure appeared once again, this time right beside his bed.

"Inverawe! Inverawe!" it repeated in a hoarse voice. "Hide him not! Blood for blood. It is the Campbell way!" Then the ghost disappeared into the blackness.

The next morning Duncan knew that he had not gone far enough. To seek the revenge the ghost wanted, he would have to kill the murderer. Duncan would have no peace until he did.

He grabbed his sword and headed off toward the cave.

But when he got there, the murderer was nowhere to be found. The food that Duncan had given him was missing too. Duncan breathed a sigh of relief. The murderer had fled. Duncan could not carry out his grisly task.

As he headed out of the cave, he came face to face with the ghost of his cousin once again. This time, the ghost was waving, as if to say good-bye. "Farewell," it moaned as it faded from sight. "Farewell, cousin, until we meet again at Ticonderoga!"

Now Duncan had never heard of Ticonderoga, and he cared little about finding out where it was. He was simply relieved that the ghost seemed to have left. He decided not to worry about whatever or wherever Ticonderoga was.

A few months later, Duncan was called out of retirement to accompany British and Scottish troops to the New World to defend British settlements against the French. This war was known as the French and Indian War. Duncan was glad to leave his homeland and to put the memory of the hideous ghost and the murdering stranger out of his mind.

Duncan was made a major with the 42nd Brigade and sailed across the ocean and then up the Hudson River. He and his men settled for a time in what is now Albany, New York, to await further orders.

Soon they were told their actual destination. First they were to advance to St. George, and then they were going to march on Fort Carillon.

The troops made their way to the French fort and made camp in the woods, waiting for the moment they would attack. As they waited, Campbell took a walk along a riverbank. Suddenly, he came face to face with the ghost that he knew to be his cousin.

"Inverawe! Inverawe!" the apparition called out. "We have met at Ticonderoga." Then, in an instant, the ghost vanished.

Ticonderoga? Duncan thought. But this place was known as Carillon. He hurried back to camp and told his commanding officer, a Colonel Grant, what he had seen.

Grant just shook his head. "Must be the stress of battle, my boy," he said in a fatherly way. "I am curious about one thing, though. How did you come to know that the Indians call this place Ticonderoga? It's simply not common knowledge."

It was then that Duncan knew his awful

fate. He would not survive the battle the next day, he was certain of it. His cousin had come back from the dead to seek his revenge, just as he had promised.

The next day 1,110 English soldiers attacked the fort. The French outnumbered them and held their position. After the battle, 306 Englishmen were dead and 316 were injured. Duncan was among the injured, but his wound was superficial. The army doctors thought he would easily recover.

Duncan knew otherwise.

Fulfilling the curse, Duncan died three days later, quickly and mysteriously, of wounds that should have easily healed. The bloodthirsty ghost of Donald Campbell had finally gotten its revenge on the man who had concealed his murderer.

The ghost of Donald Campbell still roams the halls of Fort Ticonderoga, calling "Inverawe! Inverawe! We have met at Ticonderoga." You might catch a glimpse of this Scotsman's ghost

yourself if you visit the fort in Ticonderoga, New York. Duncan Campbell is buried nearby at Union Cemetery.

THE
GHOSTLY
LADY
OF
RAYNHAM
HALL

FOR years, ghost hunters have been trying to capture the image of a ghost on film. In the late 1800s, many photographers claimed to have been successful at producing photographs of all kinds of ghostly images. In fact, "spirit photography" became all the rage.

Most of these photographs were faked, though. During the early days of photography, before people really understood how it worked, it was easy to fool people. Photographers would take a picture of one person. Then, after that person left, they used the same film to take *another picture of someone else who was supposed to be the spirit. When the film was developed, the double exposure would reveal the "spirit" standing behind the live person.*

And yet, one dark day in an old English manor back in the 1930s, a camera captured something that seemed to be from another world. It is an image that baffles photography experts to this day.

The young photographer tried to think of this trip to Raynham Hall as just another assignment. He and his assistant had been hired to take pictures of the old stone mansion in Norfolk, England, for a magazine. But Raynham Hall wasn't just another old English manor house. Raynham Hall was haunted, and even the most doubtful among the English believed in its ghost.

As he and his assistant rode into the English countryside, the photographer tried not to think about the rumors he had heard about the "Brown Lady," the ghost who haunted the manor, but he couldn't help himself. Most people thought the Brown Lady was Dorothy Walpole, the lady of the manor during the early 1700s. After she had married Lord Townshend, he discovered that she had been keeping a terrible secret from him. She had once been in love with his best friend, Lord Wharton, some years earlier. When Townshend heard this, he was so furious he locked his new wife in her room. No one knows how she died, but it was rumored that her death was bloody and violent—at the hands of her jealous husband.

The photographer shook his head, trying to rid his mind of such thoughts. Once he and his assistant arrived at the house, though, the new Lady Townshend did nothing but talk nonstop about the hauntings. She had never seen the ghost herself, she said, but many of her guests had. The photographer tried to ignore her stories and go about setting up his equipment, but she kept talking while he worked.

The first sighting of the ghost, she claimed, had happened in the early nineteenth century. King George IV had been asleep in Lady Walpole's former room when he awoke to see a woman in a brown dress standing by his bed. Her hair was in disarray and a frightfully wicked smile was on her face. He was so terrified that he left right then and there, in the middle of the night. Later, a Colonel Loftus saw her at Christmastime. He followed her down the hallway, until the image seemed to pass right through a door.

"Nonsense," the photographer muttered to himself. Still there was a bit of a nagging doubt in the back of his mind. He pushed it aside and continued to set up his photographic equipment.

Lady Townshend went on telling her story to the photographer's assistant, seeming not to care that the photographer wasn't showing any interest. The most famous sighting of the ghost, she said, happened not long after that. A Captain Marrayat had heard tales of the ghost, but he scoffed at them. In fact, he laughed out loud at the stories he heard one day while fox hunting with his friends. To prove that he wasn't frightened by "imaginary" ghosts, he begged to be allowed to sleep in the very room where the ghost had been last sighted. The lord of the manor granted permission, and

Marrayat headed up the stairs, along with his two hunting companions.

They didn't get very far. As they walked down the hallway, they saw a figure in a brown dress. She carried a lamp in her hand. Marrayat assumed she was one of the servants and moved to the side to allow her to pass. As she walked by them, she turned her face toward them. Marrayat screamed in terror. The woman's face wore a hideous grin, and in her sockets there were no eyes. Marrayat aimed his rifle at her and fired, but the bullets passed right through her. The ghostly apparition continued down the hall, turning one more time to face the three men with her evil smile and eyeless sockets.

"All ready," the photographer called, hoping that the stories would stop now that he was ready to begin shooting. He had planned to start by taking pictures of the grand staircase that led to the second floor. The photographer took several shots and then began replacing the film in his camera.

All of a sudden he heard his assistant scream. The photographer looked at his friend. His face was ghostly pale. His whole body was shaking.

"My heavens, what's the matter?" the photographer asked.

"Didn't you see it?" the assistant said. "She was, she was . . ."

"Don't be ridiculous," the photographer replied. "I didn't see a thing."

"But I saw her, the Brown Lady. She was walking down the stairs."

"Come on, old chap. It's just your imagination playing tricks on you."

"Yes, I suppose that's it," the assistant replied weakly. "All those stories kind of went to my head."

The two finished their work at the mansion and, a bit shaken, headed back to their studio to begin developing the film.

It was the photographer who turned pale this time. When he developed the photograph of the staircase, an unexpected image could clearly be seen. A woman in a long dress was descending the stairs.

He had taken the world's first photograph of a ghost.

The photograph of the Brown Lady is widely published in books about ghosts. It was examined by experts who see no way that the photograph could have been faked. If you are ever in Norfolk, England, don't forget to take a trip to Raynham Hall. But be careful about taking photographs. You never know what your camera's eye might find!

THE
EVIL
WIZARD
OF
CLIPTOWN

I T is said that the last wish of a dying person is often a sacred request. Those who witness such a request are to follow it to the letter. According to superstition, failing to do so can only bring bad luck—or worse. In some cases, the spirit of the dead person may even come back to make sure that the last wish is fulfilled. The only way to get rid of the ghost is to grant that last request.

A certain couple living in West Virginia in the late 1700s learned just how important it is to listen to a dying man's last wish. It was a lesson they never forgot.

"A night not fit for man nor beast." That's what Adam Livingstone said to his wife before they turned in on that miserable night. Cold, hard sleet was pounding down on their little farmhouse. Shaking the rafters, the wind howled through the trees in the valley.

The two really didn't expect any visitors anyway. It was true that they sometimes took in weary travelers who journeyed the Baltimore-Kentucky trail in wagons or on foot, but they were sure that there wouldn't be any travelers tonight. The weather had been too wretched lately. Parts of the trail had been completely flooded out. No one would dare travel on a night like this.

But just as they had snuffed out their candles, they heard a sharp knock at their door. It was a young traveler after all, his black cape dripping wet. Through chattering teeth, he explained that his wagon had lost its wheel somewhere down the road and that he needed shelter for the night. The Livingstone farmhouse was the only such shelter for miles around, and so Adam graciously invited him inside. After warming himself by the fire, the stranger made a bed for himself out of a few old blankets and was soon sound asleep. Adam returned to his wife's side in their oversized featherbed.

The two had been asleep for only an hour when they were awakened by a horrible scream. They looked up to see the stranger at their doorway, clutching his chest.

"I'm dying," he rasped. "You must get me a priest. I must have my last rites."

Adam looked at the young man and shook his head. The stranger looked perfectly healthy—healthier, in fact, than when he had first arrived at the house. The color was back in his cheeks and his eyes had brightened. He couldn't be dying. There was surely nothing wrong with him.

"Ah, my friend," Adam said, "you are merely tired from your journey. Go back to the fire and warm yourself. You will soon be back to your old self."

"I tell you, I am dying," cried the man. "You must fetch a priest."

Outside the wind howled even louder. By now, Adam's wife was awake, sitting bolt upright in bed.

"But in this weather, sir, you cannot expect us to go searching for a priest," Adam protested. "The nearest one is a full day's ride away, and that's in clear weather."

Adam could see that the man had tears in his eyes. "I beg you one last time," the man said. "I am dying. I need a priest."

But Adam refused him once again. The man finally returned to his place by the fire, and Adam and his wife fell back to sleep, sure that the stranger was simply weary from his journey.

The next day they found out how wrong they were. The stranger's lifeless body was stretched in front of the fire. His skin was a pale ghostly white. When Adam felt for his pulse, there was none. The man had died just as he had said he would—and without the blessing of a priest.

The stranger carried no papers with him and no one in the village seemed to know who he was. The Livingstones searched up and down the old trail looking for his wagon, but found none. The couple had no choice but to bury the man on their farm in a simple ceremony.

After they returned from the little funeral, they built a fire in the fireplace and reviewed the strange events of the last day and night. Suddenly, a flaming log jumped from the fireplace onto the hearth. Another log shot clear across the room and hit the opposite wall. The Livingstones ran to the well and got buckets of water to douse the fire. But for the rest of the day, the logs wouldn't stay in the fireplace. Adam and his wife bundled in blankets to keep warm and ate a cold supper that evening. The Livingstones got little sleep that night.

But what happened the next day was even weirder. A stagecoach driver appeared at their door and demanded to know why the two had placed a rope in front of their house, preventing his passage down the trail. The Livingstones saw no rope, but clearly the stagecoach driver did. And he could not pass through the invisible force until he used his knife to cut through it.

However, once the rope was cut, it seemed to "heal itself" and prevented others from passing by until it was cut again.

That wasn't the only weird thing that happened to the Livingstones. They also began hearing clacking sounds, as if scissors were being open and shut. Giant holes began to appear in all their clothing. When visitors and curiosity seekers came to visit the Livingstones, they too found that their clothing would be ripped and torn. The Livingstones became well-known for this supposed haunting, so well-known that their small farm was known as "Cliptown" or the "Wizard's Clip."

Then the haunting turned bloody. One day, as Mrs. Livingstone watched from the kitchen, the heads of her turkeys and chickens fell off, as if they had been chopped off by an invisible ax. That night, the Livingstones' barn burned to the ground. All the cattle inside were killed.

The Livingstones were at their wits' end. This was their home and they didn't want to leave it. But they wondered how they could live with whatever or whoever was haunting their place—especially now that the haunting had turned so destructive.

Then came the dream. On a night not unlike the stormy night that had first brought the stranger to their house, Adam Livingstone had a nightmare so vivid that he was sure it was real. First he saw a man in a black cape who looked much like the unfortunate stranger. The stranger did not speak, but Adam Livingstone heard a voice anyway. "Fetch Father Cahill. Fetch Father Cahill," the voice said. "I am dying." Then Adam saw another figure, this one wearing a priest's robe. The second figure was blessing the first.

The next day, Adam knew that he had to go in search of this Father Cahill. He saddled his horse and made the day's journey to the nearest Catholic church. There he found a priest who looked exactly like the one in his dream. He was surprised to see that the priest was already in his traveling attire.

"Ah, I've been waiting for you," the priest explained.

"Waiting for me?" Adam asked, puzzled. "But how did you know I was coming?"

"From the messenger you sent last night, of course," replied Father Cahill. "A tall gentleman in a cape. He said that you needed a priest to administer last rites."

Adam shook his head in disbelief. Could it be possible that the spirit of the stranger had arranged his own last rites?

But Adam knew that it really didn't matter who had summoned the priest. All that mattered now was that the last rites be given— quickly, before anything else happened to his home.

The two made their way back to the farm and the priest performed the sacred rites over the stranger's grave. With the dying man's last wish fulfilled, the spirit of the stranger must have finally found peace. Life on the Livingstone farm returned to its peaceful ways as well. When the Livingstones themselves died, they were so grateful to the priest that they left their land to the Catholic church.

You can still visit Cliptown near the town of Middleway, West Virginia. You can even stop by the Catholic chapel on the grounds of the old property, which is now a religious retreat. Be sure to visit only in the daytime. It is said that on certain nights, an image of a man in a black cape can be seen entering the chapel. And sometimes, the townsfolk say, they can hear the snipping and clipping sounds on the high wind.

THE
HOUSE
THAT
GHOSTS
BUILT

CAN the dead actually speak to the living? Those who believe in spiritualism say it is quite possible to make contact with the spirit world. Spiritualists believe that the spirits of the dead have much to tell us about the world of the living.

In the nineteenth century, one of the ways spiritualists claimed to be able to do this was through an elaborate ceremony called a séance. Séances were held to encourage the spirits to *communicate with the living. A person called a medium led the ceremony and called the spirit forth. Sometimes a spirit would reveal itself to everyone at the séance, but usually it was only the medium who claimed to speak directly with the deceased. Today, most people think that séances are faked, but there are some who believe strongly that the spirit world can be contacted.*

Sarah Winchester was one of those believers. And her belief led her to do something many would call crazy. Sarah couldn't help herself, though—she had to do what the ghosts told her to do. It was the only way she could cope with the evil that seemed to follow her wherever she went.

In 1881, Sarah Winchester felt as if she were the luckiest woman alive. She was deeply in love with her husband, William Winchester. Because William had inherited a great fortune from his father, the man who had invented and manufactured the Winchester rifle, the couple lived in the lap of luxury. Their home was one of the most elegant in New Haven, Connecticut. And the parties they gave were practically legendary all over the East Coast.

Sarah's life became complete when she gave birth to a daughter. Now she truly had everything she wanted—a wonderful husband, all of her material needs satisfied, and a beautiful baby.

Then Sarah's luck changed. First, her baby died only a month after she was born. Sarah would never get over the loss. She was sure that her daughter's death was the result of some evil force. Then her husband died, too. Sarah fell into deep despair. She couldn't make sense of the tragedy in her life. She was plagued by guilt, certain that she had done something to bring on her horrible misfortune.

Sarah was determined to find out why such terrible things had happened to her. She was sure that if she could only speak to her dead husband, she could find the answer. She sought the help of several mediums and attended séance after séance, but she could not make contact with her dearly departed William.

Sarah was at her wits' end when she met the famous Adam Coons, a well-known medium. Coons agreed to help Sarah Winchester—for a price, of course. Sarah didn't care how much it cost. After all, she was a rich widow. She paid Coons what he demanded and followed him into his séance room.

Candles lit the room and the smell of incense wafted through the air. Coons asked Sarah to sit across from him at a small table. He held her hands and began chanting strange words. Then he closed his eyes and began shaking for several minutes. When he opened them, he told Sarah that he had indeed spoken to her dead husband. And William Winchester had an important message for her.

According to the medium, the Winchesters were being punished by the spirits of the people who had been killed by the Winchester rifle. They had caused William's own death, as well as the death of her daughter. There was only one way to stop more horrible disasters from happening. Sarah must build the spirits a house where they would feel welcome.

Now a whole new set of questions spun through Sarah's head. Where should she build this house? What kind of house would the spirits like? How could she do it all on her own?

"Don't worry," the medium assured her. "The spirits will tell you what to do."

After the séance, Sarah took a trip across the country to search for the perfect building site. She was confident that what the medium had told her was true. When she found the right spot, the spirits would send her a message telling her so.

In the Santa Clara Valley in California, she found an eight-room farmhouse on forty-four acres of land. As soon as she laid eyes on the place, she heard a voice close to her utter the words, "This is it." Sarah knew she had found her ghost house. She bought the house from the doctor who owned it and moved all of her belongings inside.

She hadn't been there long when she heard the voices. The spirits told her to expand the house so that it would be big enough for them all. The spirits also told her exactly how they wanted it built.

For the next thirty-six years of her life, Sarah followed the instructions of the spirits and had workers tear down, rebuild, and remodel every square inch of the house. Construction experts worked day and night on the building, which eventually covered six acres. The cost of the remodeling through the years totaled about five and a half million dollars.

The spirits had strange tastes in architecture. By the time of Sarah's death in 1922, the ghost home had 160 rooms and endless stretches of corridors. It had 10,000 windows, 950 doors, 40 staircases, and 47 fireplaces. Many of the windows and doors opened not into other rooms, but into solid walls. Some of the staircases led nowhere at all. There were secret rooms and passageways throughout the strange house. All of it, Sarah claimed, was built to the specifications of the spirits of the people who had suffered death by the Winchester rifle.

At some point during the building of the house, Sarah became convinced that spirits were attracted to the number thirteen. She insisted that each room have thirteen doors, thirteen chandeliers, thirteen windows, and thirteen steps. Every night, she had a table set for thirteen in a special windowless room called the séance room. There, she claimed, she served twelve ghostly guests. In another room, the blue room, she entertained her ghostly companions at midnight, after their hearty meal.

After Sarah's death, her will, which had been signed thirteen times, left the house to her niece, provided that she always welcomed those from the spirit world as her guests. When her niece sold the house, she made the same provision to the new owners, who began to operate the house as a tourist attraction.

It is said that Sarah still visits the home she and her ghostly friends created. On one occasion, a staff member saw a woman in an old-fashioned dress sitting at a kitchen table. She didn't pay much attention to the woman. After all, the staff was always putting on special events. This woman was probably involved in one of them.

It was only after she checked with other staff members that she learned the truth about the figure. There was no promotion or special event going on in the house, no reason that anyone should be in costume. The woman had come face-to-face with the spirit of Sarah

Winchester, who had come back to her old home for a ghostly visit.

You can tour the strange Winchester House and its grounds in San Jose, California, and decide for yourself whether Sarah Winchester was acting on ghostly advice when she built it. But don't be surprised to find many of the rooms sealed. There are some who feel that the house's spirits may still lurk behind those closed doors and that they are best left undisturbed.

THE
GHOSTLY
MONK
OF
ELM
VICARAGE

TERRIBLE *mistakes, unfortunate over-sights, horrible misunderstandings—such things happen in the course of everyday living. Evidently, many spirits feel it is necessary to make up for whatever shortcomings they had while they were living. A ghost may spend eternity trying to correct some sort of wrong that he committed during his earthly life.*

When that wrong is so great that it results in some kind of disaster, the ghost may need to take great pains to make up for it. Such was the case with Ignatius the Bell Ringer, a spirit doomed to walk the earth until he made up for his one horrible mistake. In a small village in England, he found a way to right the wrong, but before it was all over, one young woman would have to spend a night in terror.

From the moment the Reverend and Mrs. Bradshaw moved into the residence known as the Elm Vicarage, things were not quite right. Both the minister and his young wife heard footsteps and strange tappings at all hours of the day and night. They could not find the source of the noises. Their home was a new one and it was sturdy in the wind. Besides, the noises didn't sound like ones that a house makes as it settles or that the wind causes as it blows through the trees. These sounded exactly like footsteps, sharp and distinct.

Although her husband continued to look for a reasonable explanation for the sounds, Mrs. Bradshaw was convinced that they were being made by a ghostly spirit of some sort. She had read many books about ghosts and believed that they existed. They weren't always evil, she was quick to remind her husband. Some ghosts, she insisted, were friendly ones, and that was exactly the feeling she was getting about the ghost in this house.

Her feelings about the "thing" that was haunting the vicarage were confirmed just weeks later. As she walked down a narrow hallway, she felt her sleeve brush against something. When she looked up, she saw the faint outline of a man dressed in a brown sack-like dress. The man wore a little brown skullcap on his head. The outline became darker and darker in front of the startled Mrs. Bradshaw's eyes.

Then the figure turned to her and spoke. Instead of whispering some evil spell, it spoke these simple words, "Please, do be careful." Then it slowly turned away.

Mrs. Bradshaw was now certain that the ghost meant her no harm and so she called out to it, "Who are you?"

"Ignatius the Bell Ringer," the apparition replied and then slowly faded out of sight.

Mrs. Bradshaw was delighted. Not only was

her ghost friendly, but it actually had a name! For the next few weeks, she spent every waking hour at the town's old library researching her ghost. Her husband scoffed at her efforts, sure her imagination had run away with her. There was no ghost, he insisted, and she was wasting her time with all this silly nonsense.

But Mrs. Bradshaw was determined to find out where her ghostly visitor came from. First she tried to track down the name Ignatius. Then she looked up information about old monasteries and about Christianity throughout England's history. She discovered a couple of interesting things. The brown dress the figure wore, for instance, was exactly like the garb that monks wore in the fifteenth century.

Next Mrs. Bradshaw decided to research the land on which the vicarage stood. That's when she found her answer.

Several hundred years before, a monastery had been built on the very spot where the Bradshaws' house now stood. The monastery lay near a river that tended to flood. In modern times, a flood wall had been built to protect the property. But there had been no such structure to protect the monastery. So

Ignatius, one of the monks living in the monastery, had a special job to do. He was to watch for rising floodwaters and warn the other monks by ringing a bell so all could head for higher ground. Ignatius had carried out his task successfully many times—until one night when he fell asleep on his job. The rains came and the waters rose. The monastery was swept away in the torrent and a number of the monks drowned. Ignatius was one of the survivors, but he spent the rest of his life in disgrace for his careless actions. It was only by doing penance, or performing a good deed, that he could relieve himself of blame. But Ignatius died of some mysterious disease before he could perform that special penance.

For some reason, the whole idea of the penance made Mrs. Bradshaw uneasy. The notion of a ghost in her house didn't bother her. In fact, she enjoyed Ignatius. She saw him roaming the halls during the time she was doing the research. Of course, her husband laughed off her story once again, but she knew what she had seen.

Now she knew something else about Ignatius. He had come back to do something, to perform some penance so that he would be forgiven for letting the monks die. And for some reason, that made Mrs. Bradshaw's heart pound. Could it be, she wondered, that the penance had something to do with her? Could it be that the monk's warning to be careful had sinister implications?

Mrs. Bradshaw would know the answer soon enough. One night, she slept in the guest room because her husband had a bad cold. Because she was lonely, she tried to coax her terrier into the room with her. Usually happy to snuggle beside her, the terrier wouldn't budge. In fact, it growled and snarled at the doorway to the room. Finally, she coaxed the dog in with a dog biscuit, but it took him a while to settle down. Eventually, the two were sleeping soundly.

Suddenly, Mrs. Bradshaw was awakened by a powerful throbbing sensation in her neck. Her dog was barking wildly. The sensation made her choke. In terror, she realized she was being strangled by some invisible force. As she struggled, something even more horrible happened. A vague dark shape, a sort of cloud, hovered above her. And from that cloud, two bony hands dripping with blood clutched at her neck. The force they exerted on her neck became stronger and stronger until she was sure that she faced certain death.

Then, from a dark corner of the room, she saw the image of Ignatius in his brown monk's robe approach her. He reached forward and grabbed the bloody hands. As Mrs. Bradshaw choked, he tried to pull the hands from her neck. The hands only drew tighter and Mrs. Bradshaw could not breathe. Finally, in one huge forceful movement, Ignatius pulled the hands back. Then both the monk and the strange dark shape disappeared.

As soon as she was able to, Mrs. Bradshaw ran screaming from the room to find her husband. Breathlessly, she told him her unbelievable story. At first he didn't believe her, but when she pulled the collar of her nightgown down, there was no mistaking what was there. A ring of bruises circled her neck and drops of dark red blood, still wet, shone from her collarbone. Now her husband had to admit that something had happened in that room, something that had almost taken her life. And, if her story was true, Ignatius the Bell

Ringer had come to her rescue.

It would be some time before Mrs. Bradshaw would feel up to doing much of anything. She insisted that her husband board up the room where she had been attacked, thinking that would stop whatever was in there from invading the rest of her house. But after a few weeks, she felt well enough to take a walk by herself in the garden. It was there that she saw Ignatius again.

In a quiet voice, he explained to her that a murder had occurred on the very spot where the room had been built. The murderer's evil spirit had come back from the dead to claim yet one more victim. As horrible as the incident had been for her, Ignatius gently explained, it had allowed him to perform his penance for the lost monks. Now his soul could rest. He told her she needn't fear that the murderer's spirit would come back. It had returned to whatever horrible place it came from.

As Ignatius's image began to fade from sight, Mrs. Bradshaw felt strangely sad. "Will I see you again?" she asked the apparition.

"Listen for the bell! Listen for the bell!" was Ignatius's only reply.

When the Bradshaws were well up in years, they heard the bell in their bell tower ring three times. In just three short days, the minister died of a heart attack. A year later, Mrs. Bradshaw heard the bell, and this time she knew that it tolled for her. Soon she would meet her favorite monk once again.

You can still visit the famous bell tower of Elm Vicarage south of Wisbech in Cambridgeshire, England. No one has seen an image of Ignatius since the incident with Mrs. Bradshaw. But it is said that the bell in the tower still tolls three times mysteriously to tell the village of an impending death.

ABOUT THE AUTHOR

There is nothing Tracey Dils likes better than a good ghost story. When she was growing up, she loved to scare her friends and family with terrifying tales of haunted places. In fact, she scared her little sister so badly that to this day she still sleeps with the lights on!

Tracey has never actually seen a ghost, but she has seen evidence of one. She was having lunch at an old inn in her hometown. The inn was said to be haunted. While she was eating, a tray of salt and pepper shakers rose off a counter, hung in midair for a few seconds, and then fell to the floor in one big crash. Tracey thinks that a ghost was trying to get her attention so that she'd write a story about it.

When she's not writing or spending time with her husband, Richard, and her two children, Emily and Phillip, Tracey loves to talk to young people about writing. She has held ghost-story writing workshops in schools, libraries, and writing centers throughout her home state.

Tracey is also the author of *The Scariest Stories You've Ever Heard, Part III*, as well as several picture books, including *Annabelle's Awful Waffle* and *A Look Around Coral Reefs*.